CW00392178

THE LIFE THAT I HAVE

Leo Marks

Illustrated by
Elena Gaussen Marks

SOUVENIR PRESS

Leo Marks was in charge of codes for the Resistance Movement when he wrote the poem 'The Life That I Have'.

On Christmas Eve 1943 he learned that his fiancée Ruth had been killed in a plane crash in Canada. He went up to the roof of the building where he worked and, 'Looking up at God's pavement for signs of new pedestrians, I transmitted a message to her which I'd failed to deliver when I had the chance'.*

In 1944 he gave the poem to a French Resistance worker, Violette Szabo, to use as a code as he 'didn't think that Ruth would mind'. It has since become one of the most popular love poems in the English language.

In 1966 Leo married the artist and portrait painter Elena Gaussen who has illustrated this book.

* From Leo Marks' memoirs of his years with SOE, *Between Silk and Cyanide* (HarperCollins, 1998).

violetta szabo

The life that I have

Leo Marks.

Is all that I have

Chiswick Mall.

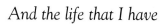

And the life that I have

Is yours.

Norgeby HOUSE

The love that I have

Leo Marks &
Elena Gaussen Marks

Of the life that I have

Hayling Island.

Is yours and yours and yours.

Albert Memorial.

A sleep I shall have

Sawston, Cambs.,

A rest I shall have

S. Croce Florence

Yet death will be but a pause.

Gers, France

For the peace of my years

kew bridge

In the long green grass

long-melford

Will be yours and yours

St Jory de Chalais

and yours.

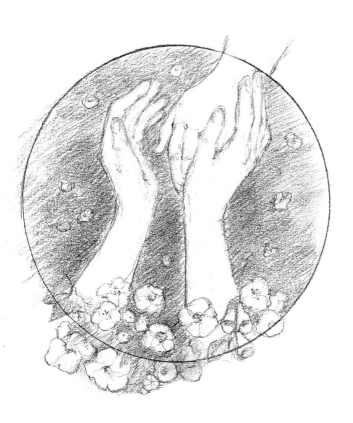

This edition first published 1999 by Souvenir Press Ltd,
43 Great Russell Street, London WC1B 3PA

ISBN 0 285 63532 8

Reprinted and bound by Bath Press